A *Doonesbury* book

Gotta Run, My Government Is Collapsing

Selected Cartoons from
He's Never Heard of You, Either, Vol. 2

FAWCETT CREST • NEW YORK

Gotta Run, My Government Is Collapsing

© B Trudeau

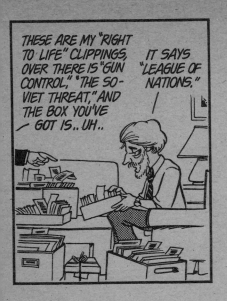

..AND WHILE IT'S TRUE THAT SOME OF MY CLIPPINGS FROM "LIBERTY" AND "COLLIER'S" ARE A BIT DATED, MOST OF THEM HAVE AS MUCH SIGNIFICANCE FOR US NOW AS THEY DID IN THE '30's.

FOR EXAMPLE, DID YOU KNOW THIS? "STUDIES NOW SHOW THAT NEARLY 95% OF ALL PEOPLE ON THE PUBLIC DOLE ROUTINELY TURN DOWN HONEST WORK WHEN IT IS OFFERED TO THEM."

MR. FORD WAS OUT ON THE LINKS ONE DAY WHEN HIS GOLF CART BROKE DOWN. HE DECIDED TO HOOF IT. AT THE END OF THE DAY, HE FOUND THAT NOT ONLY HAD HE SHOT 18 HOLES OF GOLF, BUT HE'D ALSO ACQUIRED A ROSY TAN!

AT THE SAME TIME?

IT WAS SOMETHING OF A BREAK-THROUGH.

REVEREND SLOAN, I CAN PERSONALLY ASSURE YOU THAT THE HOSTAGES ARE STILL IN PERFECT PHYSICAL AND MENTAL HEALTH.

BUT AS A MAN OF GOD, YOU SHOULD BE AWARE OF THE STATE OF MORAL TURPITUDE WHICH EXISTS AMONG YOUR COUNTRYMEN..

GB Trudeau

HELLO?

REVEREND SLOAN? THIS IS PRESIDENT BANI SADR.

MR. PRESIDENT! BOY, AM I GLAD TO HEAR FROM YOU, SIR. WHEN AM I GOING TO GET TO SEE THE HOSTAGES?

ANY DAY NOW, REVEREND. AS SOON AS WE CAN MAKE ARRANGEMENTS..

I'D RUN YOU OVER TO SEE THEM MYSELF, BUT IT LOOKS LIKE I'M GOING TO BE TIED UP ALL WEEK.

DOING WHAT, SIR?

CLINGING TO POWER. BUT MONDAY FOR SURE, OKAY?

"AS TALESE EMERGED FROM HIS '57 TRIUMPH, HIS EYES LOOKED UP HUNGRILY AT THE FLICKERING RED NEON SIGN THAT READ 'LIVE NUDE CO-EDS'.."

"HE BOUNDED UP THE THREE FLIGHTS OF STEPS, ANXIOUS TO KEEP HIS APPOINTMENT WITH THE VOLUPTUOUS CHEMISTRY MAJOR WHOSE PHOTO HE HAD SELECTED WITH SUCH CARE FROM THE MASSAGE PARLOR PICTURE BOOK."

"WHEN THEY WERE FINALLY ALONE TALESE TURNED TO HER AND SAID, 'I WANT TO JOIN YOUR SILENT REVOLUTION OF THE SENSES, YOUR DEPARTURE FROM CONVENTIONALITY.' THE MASSEUSE SMILED AND REACHED FOR THE POWDER."

"MEANWHILE, OUT IN THE CAR, TALESE'S WIFE WAS GROWING IMPATIENT.."

UNDERSTANDABLY!

"TALESE WENT UPSTAIRS WITH THREE OF HIS FELLOW REVOLUTIONARIES, AND FOR THE NEXT SEVERAL HOURS FLOUTED CONVENTION. SO PREOCCUPIED DID HE BECOME WITH HIS SILENT PROTEST AGAINST THE CENSORS AND CLERICS, HE FAILED TO HEAR A KNOCK."

"TALESE LOOKED UP TO SEE FOUR MORE PIONEERS."

HARDY STOCK, I HOPE.